# LIFT
# OFF

# Donovan Livingston

# LIFT OFF

## From the Classroom to the Stars

Foreword by **WES MOORE**

**SPIEGEL & GRAU**

NEW YORK

Published in the United States by Spiegel & Grau, an
imprint of Random House, a division of Penguin Random
House LLC, New York.

SPIEGEL & GRAU and Design is a registered trademark of
Penguin Random House LLC.

*Lift Off* was first presented as a convocation address given
by the author at the Harvard Graduate School of Education
graduation ceremony, May 25, 2016.

ISBN 978-0-399-59137-2
Ebook ISBN 978-0-399-59138-9

Printed in the United States of America on acid-free paper

randomhousebooks.com
spiegelandgrau.com

9 8 7 6 5 4 3 2 1

*Book design by Simon M. Sullivan*

*To my darling wife, Lauren—*
*my lemon-pepper, bacon-wrapped,*
*pan-seared, filet-o-fresh,*
*butter-pecan, honey-dipped,*
*angel-winged, halo-wearing*
*ebony empress—for whom*
*my love is forever ascending*

# FOREWORD

## by WES MOORE

Donovan Livingston was chosen by his peers at the Harvard Graduate School of Education to deliver the convocation address at their graduation ceremony on May 25, 2016. As soon as he began speaking, the rest of the world understood why: the power of his message, the preciseness of his spoken words, the clarity of his belief in both the educators who lead our schools and the students who will become our future leaders. In that moment, hearing those words, we understood our shared cause in the importance of education as a path toward equality.

As soon as the speech was posted online, it went viral. By the end of the first week, more than thirteen million people had seen what the audience in Harvard experienced that afternoon. That was how I first came to hear his words. And I have not been the same since.

I related to Donovan's struggles; in my own world, growing up in Baltimore, I'd understood the importance of higher education, but the road map for how to accomplish my goals had been unclear. I feared that I didn't belong, and even as I progressed through academia, I believed that I was less than worthy, that my presence in university halls felt more like a social experiment than a birthright. After I graduated from Johns Hopkins and Oxford University, I realized that it wasn't the coursework that had been the greatest challenge but overcoming impostor syndrome and breaking through the psychology of impossible excellence, the notion that some unachievable bar of perfection existed, one that would always be too high for me to reach.

On the other side of those experiences, I now give back, working in education and running a platform called BridgeEdU. At Bridge we address the college-completion crisis by reinventing the freshman year of college. I see, every day, the trials so many students face as they try to make sense of a journey that for some requires wading through uncharted waters, since many of our students are the first in their families to go to college.

We need our students to win, but I am not naïve about the challenges ahead. I understand how difficult it is to make our educational system more accessible and to make completion more attainable for all students. In the end, like Donovan, we are committed to encouraging the spark in every student, and his speech reminds us why we do this work.

Though Donovan's words have already been shared around the world, I celebrate him and cherish his contributions not for his celebrity but for his sincerity. That's how he uses his gift to remind others of their own. That's how he reminds our teachers how to fight, and our students that they are worth fighting for. Donovan makes us feel ever powerful, and the truth is, we are.

Many have wondered where Donovan will end up, what he will do next. I can tell you that from what he has shared with us already, he will never be forgotten. I am sure you will find his words as timeless and inspiring as I did.

# LIFT
# OFF

*Education, then,*

*beyond all other devices of human origin,*

*is the great equalizer of the conditions of men.*

—HORACE MANN, 1848

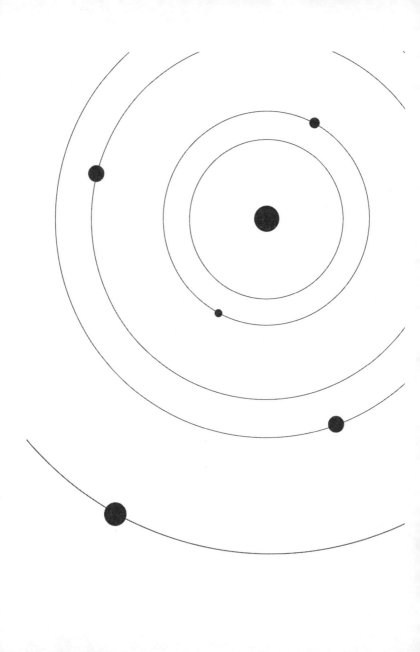

At the time of his remarks

I couldn't read—couldn't write.

Any attempt to do so,

punishable by death.

For generations we have known

of knowledge's infinite power.

Yet somehow,

we've never questioned

the keeper of the keys—

the guardians of information.

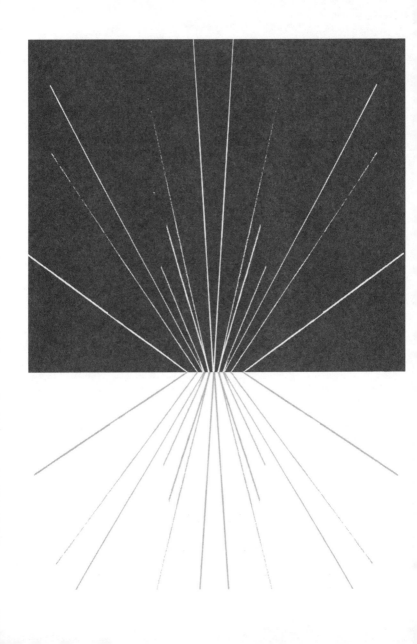

Unfortunately,

I've seen more dividing and conquering

in this order of operations—

a heinous miscalculation of reality.


For some,

the only difference

between a plantation

and a classroom

is time.

How many times

must we be made

to feel like quotas—

like tokens in coined phrases?

"Diversity."

"Inclusion."

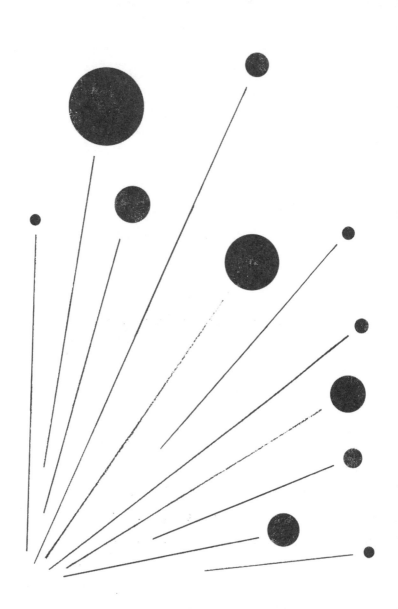

There are days

I feel like one,

like only—

a lonely blossom

in a briar patch

of broken promises.

But I've always been a thorn

in the side of injustice.

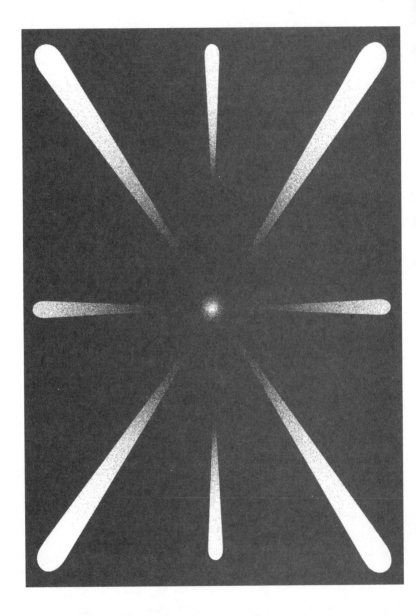

Disruptive. Talkative. A distraction.

With a passion that transcends

the confines of my consciousness—

beyond their curriculum,

beyond their standards.

I stand here,

a manifestation of love and pain,

with veins pumping revolution.

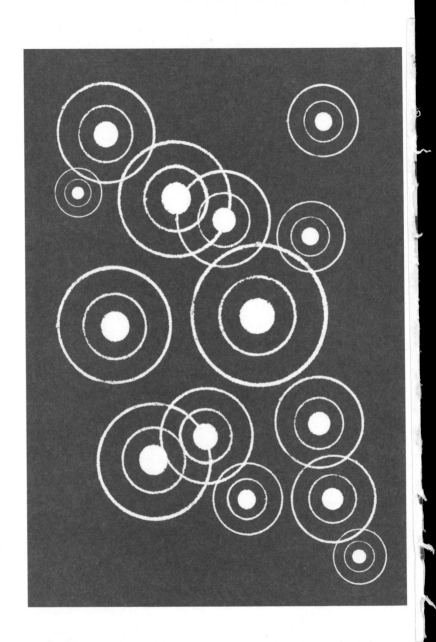

I am the strange fruit

that grew too ripe for the poplar tree.

I am a DREAM Act,

dream deferred incarnate.

I am a movement—

an amalgam of memories

America would care to forget.

My past won't allow me to sit still.

So my body, like the mind,

cannot be contained.

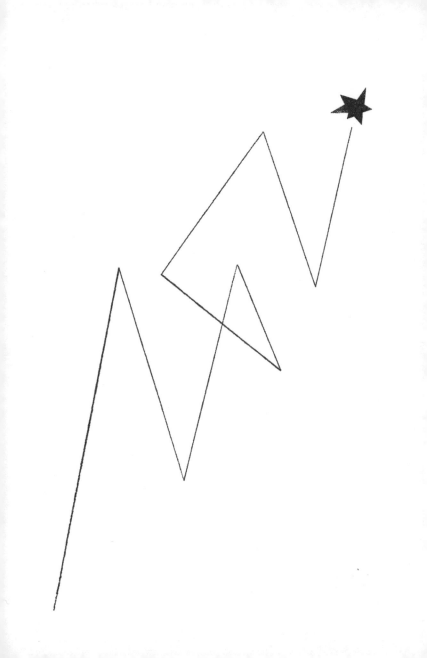

So climb and grab them.

Keep climbing. Grab them.

Spill your emotions into the Big Dipper,

pour out your soul and light up the world.

As leaders, rather than raising your voices

over the rustling of our chains,

take them off.

Uncuff us.

So we can be unencumbered by the

    lumbering weight

of poverty and privilege,

policy and ignorance.

I was in the seventh grade
when Ms. Parker told me,
"Donovan, we can put your
excess energy to good use!"
And she introduced me
to the sound of my own voice.

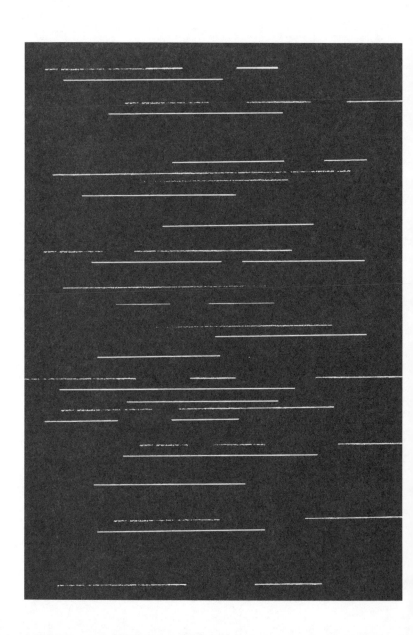

She gave me a stage. A platform.

She told me that our stories are ladders

that make it easier for us to touch the stars.

To educate requires Galileo-like patience.

Today, when I look my students in the eyes,

all I see are constellations.

If you take the time to connect the dots,

you can plot the true shape of their genius—

shining even in their darkest hour.

I look each of my students in the eyes,

and see the same light

that aligned Orion's Belt

and the pyramids of Giza.

I see the same twinkle

that guided Harriet to freedom.

I see *them.*

Beneath their masks and mischief

exists an authentic frustration,

an enslavement

to their standardized assessments.

At the core,

none of us were meant to be common.

We were born to be comets,

darting across space and time—

leaving our mark

as we crash into everything.

A crater is a reminder

that something amazing happened here—

an indelible impact

that shook up the world.

After all, educators are astronomers—

searching for the next shooting star.

I teach in hopes of turning content
into rocket ships,
tribulations into telescopes.
So a child can see their true potential
from right where they stand.

An injustice

is telling them they are stars,

without acknowledging

the night that surrounds them.


Injustice is telling them

education is the key,

while you continue

to change the locks.

Education is no equalizer—

until we acknowledge the prejudice

pervading the policies that silence me.

Until then, it is the sleep that precludes the

American Dream.

So wake up—wake up!

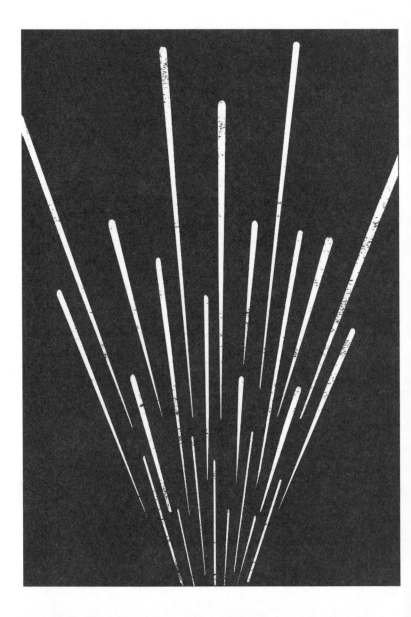

Lift your voices

until you've patched every hole

in a child's broken sky.

Wake up every child

so they know of their celestial potential.

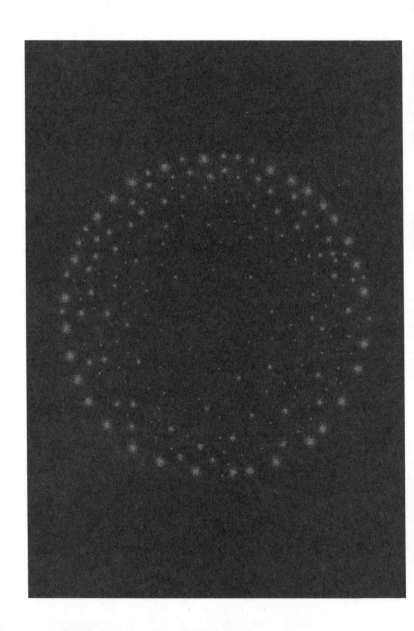

I've been a Black hole

in the classroom for far too long,

absorbing everything

without allowing my light to escape.

But those days are done.


I belong among the stars.

And so do you.

And so do they.

Together, we can inspire

galaxies of greatness

for generations to come.

No.

Sky is not the limit.

It is only the beginning.


Lift off.

DONOVAN LIVINGSTON is an award-winning educator and public speaker. His Harvard Graduate School of Education convocation address went viral, reaching more than thirteen million views, and was praised by Hillary Clinton. Livingston and his speech have been featured on CNN, NPR, the BBC, *Good Morning America,* and by news outlets across Europe, Australia, India, and South Africa. He holds master's degrees from Columbia and Harvard universities, and he has now returned to his home state as a doctoral candidate studying education at the University of North Carolina in Greensboro.

Facebook.com/dlive87
Twitter: @DLive87
Instagram: @dlive87